MEDICAL SCIENCE NOW

The first doctor whose name we know is Imhotep. He was an ancient Egyptian who lived and worked in what is now Cairo, about 4,700 years ago. He left guidelines on how to mend broken bones, clean wounds and tackle tumours. The ailments doctors treat have changed little since that time, but medical science has changed beyond all recognition – and it will keep on changing.

What is happening?

The first thing a doctor does is figure out what is wrong with a patient. This is called diagnosis and has been practised since the days of Imhotep. In the 5th century BCE, a Greek doctor called Hippocrates realised it was also important to know the prognosis – what is likely to happen to the patient. Hippocrates is said to be the founding father of medicine. Even today, all doctors swear the Hippocratic Oath, promising to use their medical knowledge ethically and honestly.

Helpful chemicals

A medicine is a chemical that works with the body to fight off diseases. The science of medicines is called pharmacology, and pharmacologists are experts in how medicines work. The first medicines were made from leaves and bark. Amazingly, even today modern medicines are based on chemicals that are found in nature, especially plants and fungi.

FUTURE TECH FOR YOU!

WHAT'S NEXT FOR MEDICINE?

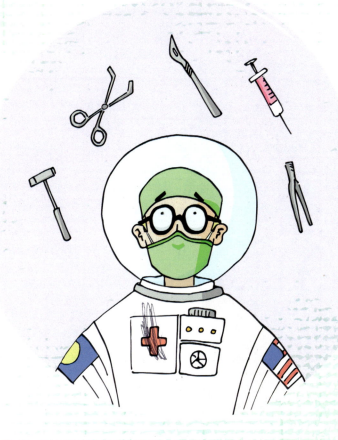

Tom Jackson

WAYLAND

First published in paperback in 2015 by Wayland

Copyright © Wayland 2015

Dewey classification: 610
ISBN: 978 0 7502 8366 3
Library eBook ISBN: 978 0 7502 8664 0
10 9 8 7 6 5 4 3 2 1

Senior editor: Julia Adams
Designer: Maddox Philpot
Illustrator: Maddox Philpot
Consultant: Sean Connolly

Picture acknowledgements:
p. 9 (top): Damien Lovegrove/
Science Photo Library; p. 15
(centre): John Rogers/University
of Illinois at Urbana-Champaign;
p. 24 (top): Fiorenzo Omenetto/
Tufts University

Wayland, an imprint of
Hachette Children's Group
Part of Hodder & Stoughton
Carmelite House
50 Victoria Embankment
London EC4Y 0DZ

Printed in China

An Hachette UK Company

www.hachette.co.uk

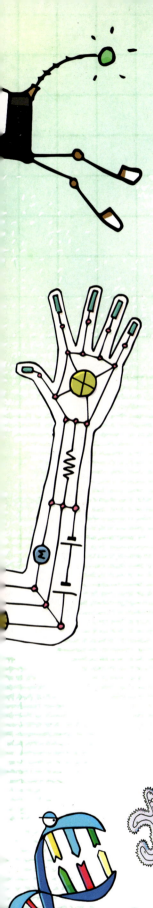
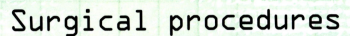

Surgical procedures

Sometimes the best thing to do is cut into the body in order to mend a body part or cut it out completely. This is obviously a difficult and dangerous job. However, that did not stop members of ancient civilisations from performing brain surgery! Skulls that are 8,000 years old have been found with holes drilled in them. This form of surgery is known as trepanning. People believed that cutting the hole would release demons — or at least cure headaches.

Into the future

Diagnosis, medicine and surgery are still the main subjects of medical science today, but in future doctors will be more likely to use computers to detect problems in the body, They will also unleash an array of high-tech gadgets that work on or even inside the body, and medicines will be fine-tuned to work perfectly for each patient. But will future science do away with doctors themselves?

In this book we'll look at the latest research and scientific developments, and explore how they might change the way we live in the years to come. An icon next to each technology we introduce will give you an idea of when it may become part of our daily lives.

GOING TO THE DOCTOR

When you are ill, the best thing to do is go to the doctor, and that will never change. However, in future, medical sensors on your body will make the appointment for you. They will then notify you of your appointment via email or text message. And when you get to see the doctor, it may not even be a person at all!

Doctor doctor, you're a computer!

10 YEARS

A doctor uses your symptoms as clues as to what is causing your illness. This is called diagnosis. One day we might be diagnosed by a computer. You will tell it your symptoms and a camera will scan the body (it might look in your mouth – say aah!). The computer will then compare your symptoms against a database of illnesses that has been set up by human doctors. Unlike a human doctor, however, a supercomputing medic can diagnose hundreds of people all at the same time.

PAUSE FOR THOUGHT

Computers are very good at recording information and following instructions but does that mean a robot doctor will never make a mistake? And what happens if the computer does get something wrong? Whose fault would it be?

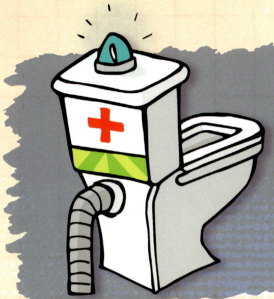

Toilet checker

In the future, wee and poo could save your life. Sensors will be included in toilets, in order to give you a health check every time you answer the call of nature. The toilet could advise you to change your diet, arrange a doctor's appointment for a minor ailment – or call an ambulance in an emergency.

PLAYING DOCTORS

5 YEARS

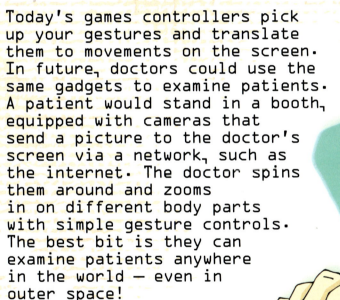

Today's games controllers pick up your gestures and translate them to movements on the screen. In future, doctors could use the same gadgets to examine patients. A patient would stand in a booth, equipped with cameras that send a picture to the doctor's screen via a network, such as the internet. The doctor spins them around and zooms in on different body parts with simple gesture controls. The best bit is they can examine patients anywhere in the world — even in outer space!

⚠ ERROR ALERT

Blood letting

Around 300 years ago, doctors thought that some illnesses were caused by too much blood in the body, and so they cut patients to let some of it out. We now know that this is almost always a terrible idea – US president George Washington was bled five times in eight hours for a sore throat, and it was probably what killed him. However, scientists have recently discovered that blood letting can help reduce symptoms caused by obesity (being very overweight), so it may become a treatment again in future.

TAKING MEDICINE

People have been taking medicines for thousands of years, starting with herbs and crushed up minerals. These did not always work, and scientists have been trying to improve medicines ever since. In future, making better medicines will not just be about finding new chemicals, but also inventing ways of getting them to where they are needed.

HOT GOLD

15 YEARS

Cancer is a growth in the body that is made up of bundles of cells. Killing cancer cells is quite easy – the big problem is finding ways of not killing the healthy cells around the cancer at the same time. Cancer cells have markers on their surface, which drugs of the future will be able to lock onto. But what then? One idea is to make a medicine that attaches tiny particles of gold to the cancer cells. Once they are in place, doctors shine infrared light (a kind of heat ray) onto the body. The gold particles absorb the heat, and literally fry the cancer – but leave the healthy cells alone.

Deadly lifesaver

12 YEARS

The black mamba is one of the most dangerous snakes in the world. Its bite can kill a person in less than an hour. So how would you feel if a doctor gave you a medicine made from black mamba venom? Scientists are investigating if proteins in the venom could work as a strong painkiller for people with serious injuries.

Powder power

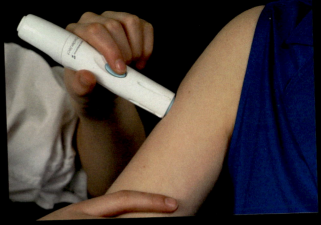

5 YEARS

No one likes getting injections, but sometimes medicine only works if it is delivered straight into the blood or muscles. In future, we won't use painful needles. Instead, a powder will be blasted through the skin using a shot of high-pressure air. The high pressure jiggles the powder around so it flows like a liquid, and the syringe can be set to push medicine to exactly the right depth in the skin, so none of it is wasted.

Once the needleless syringe is pressed against the skin, powdered drugs get injected into the body at the press of a button.

SOUNDING OFF

10 YEARS

Have you ever wondered what happens to a pill once you swallow it? It gets broken down by the stomach's juices and some of its chemicals will pass into the blood and begin to affect the body. The stomach has trouble absorbing many drugs; these have to be injected instead — ouch. One day we might just swallow ultrasonic pills. These give out waves of high-pitched sound (we can't hear it) which briefly change the stomach lining, allowing the medicines to pass through.

!ERROR ALERT

Adding juice

Having grapefruit or grapefruit juice is not always healthy. It can change the way some medicines, such as those taken for high blood pressure, work. Some chemicals in grapefruits can enhance the effects of the medicine, meaning it works too hard. This results in the same effect as an overdose. However, the same effect might be put to use one day in making cancer medicines more powerful: taking smaller, safer doses in combination with grapefruit will work just as well as a larger dose taken on its own.

GETTING A BETTER LOOK

It used to be that medics could only guess what was happening inside the body. Then, in 1816, a French doctor rolled up some paper into a tube which helped him listen to a patient's heart, and the stethoscope was born. Since then, doctors have developed several ways of scanning the inside of the body. But they are always on the look out for a better view.

Internal video

`5 YEARS`

Some cameras are designed to be inserted into your body. Doctors check the health of stomach and guts with an endoscope — a tiny video camera on the tip of a flexible probe. Not surprisingly, this is unpleasant for the patient. One day it might be possible to video your intestines using a camera in a pill. Just press record, swallow and wait for nature to take its course!

Magnetised body

`5 YEARS`

The MPI (magnetic particle imaging) scanner will one day make our blood magnetic to show if there are blockages in your heart and blood vessels. Nanoparticles of iron oxide, billions of times smaller than a grain of sand, will be injected into the blood, and the MPI will make them into tiny magnets. Their magnetism can be tracked as they travel around the body, through the heart, brain — anywhere you want to look. This could help prevent heart attacks.

Golden ruler

15 YEARS

The viruses that cause disease are too small to see clearly with microscopes that use light. Instead, scientists view them using beams of electrons (in an electron microscope). However, this freezes them in time, so you can see what they look like, but not what they do. In future, tiny rulers made of minute particles of gold could be used to reflect electrons onto viruses as they work. Ripples of electrons around the virus would measure how it is changing shape as it attacks a body. That will help medics create new vaccines.

HD scans

10 YEARS

A doctor who scans the body is called a radiologist. They are experts in figuring out what an X-ray or other scan shows. Unfortunately, an X-ray image is seldom very clear. In future, the technology used in cinema special-effects could be used to convert medical scans into crystal clear, colourful images. By putting on 3-D glasses, medics can see the inside of the body as if the skin wasn't there.

STACKS OF FACTS

X-ray:
Invisible radiation, called X-rays, passes through soft body parts, such as the skin, but not hard ones such as the bones. An X-ray image is really the outline of your skeleton.

CT (computed tomography):
A computer puts dozens of scans of the body together to produce a cross-section or 'slices' of the body.

MRI (magnetic resonance imaging):
A huge magnet and a blast of radio waves through the body make the water inside (the body is mostly water) wobble. This wobble is picked up and used to create a picture of the soft, watery body parts.

REPLACEMENT PARTS

Try as they might, doctors cannot heal every part of a patient's body. In some extreme cases, body parts may have to be amputated (removed). The obvious thing to do is replace what's missing with an artificial part, or prosthetic. This is not a new idea: ancient Egyptians used wooden prosthetics. However, in future, replacement body parts will be as good as the real thing, or perhaps even better!

10 YEARS

Mind control

Scientists are making prosthetic arms and legs that are taught to move in the same way that a baby learns to control its body. Our brains learned to control our limbs when we were young and to do it automatically. Future prosthetics will be controlled by a brain scanner that picks up brain activity and transmits commands to motors in the prosthetic. The system must be trained to recognise the correct brain waves first, but a person's prosthetic will soon move on its own – without them really thinking about it.

Superhero muscles

15 YEARS

Spiderman only exists in comics and movies, but one day real-life spiders could be the superheroes that help paralysed people walk. People are paralysed because their nerves have become disconnected. Doctors cannot reconnect them, so one idea is to put in a whole new muscle system – made from spider silk. Natural muscle is made up of tiny fibres that can shrink, or contract. A spider silk muscle contracts when it becomes damp – and has the added advantage of being stronger than steel.

CAPTAIN CYBORG

15 YEARS

Kevin Warwick is a cyborg — a cyber organism — part man, part machine. The machine part is only very small. It is a tiny chip that the British professor implanted in his arm ten years ago. The chip is connected to the nerves that control his hand and it sends out radio signals that match the electric pulses moving his fingers. This means Dr Warwick, or Captain Cyborg as he is known, can control machines with the radio signals emitted when he moves his hand — and he can do it through the internet, working robots on the other side of the world!

PAUSE FOR THOUGHT

Being a cyborg might help with medical problems, but is it a good idea to add computer components for other reasons, such as to make you stronger or cleverer? Would some people to gain unfair advantage by having these features?

CUTTING IN

In the old days, people went to the barbers to have wounds stitched and broken bones set, so the first surgeons were hairdressers. Only later did these 'surgeons' become doctors as well. In future our surgeons might not be doctors either, but robots and computers.

Sat nav for brains

5 YEARS

Brain surgery is a delicate business. Often the problem area is buried under healthy parts of the brain – one wrong move and an essential part of the brain could be damaged. In future, expert surgeons will have help finding a safe route deep into the brain, thanks to a navigation computer. The system uses brain scans to plot a route through the patient's head, so it navigates around crucial blood vessels and nerves.

Turn left at right eyeball!

Sonic Screwdriver

10 YEARS

Doctor Who might not be the only one with a sonic screwdriver in years to come. Surgeons might use them too. Scientists are developing a way of making objects spin and wobble around using pulses of sound (way too high for us to hear). In future, this sonic system could be used to massage or adjust tissue deep in the body without having to cut inside it.

Robot surgeon

NOW!

Most surgery is relatively safe, although understandably most people are nervous about operations. How would you feel if it was all done automatically by a robot? Is that better or worse? Certain operations are already carried out by robots, with every cut and slice programmed in advance. A mechanical surgeon can cut more precisely than a human and only needs to make tiny holes to get inside the body.

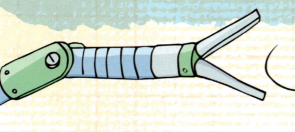

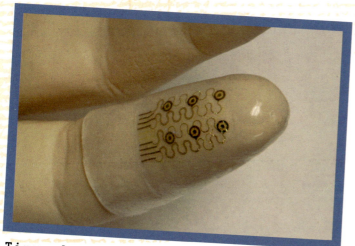

Tiny electronic circuits in the surgical 'smart tips' stimulate the wearer's nerves.

Tingle tips

5 YEARS

A surgeon's hands are highly advanced tools. One day supersensitive touch pads on a surgeon's fingertips might make them even better. The pads create a tingle in the skin when they touch something, making it easier for surgeons to feel soft and slippery innards while wearing their protective gloves. The pads could also heat up, allowing the surgeon to scorch away bad tissue with their fingertips.

! ERROR ALERT

Theatrical event

Have you every wondered why surgeons work in operating theatres? In the old days an operation was a performance with a large audience watching. Doctors did not realise that all the open wounds and blood caused dangerous infections that killed many of their patients. Not until the 1840s did doctors even realise that washing their hands between surgeries would help patients survive. Today's operating theatres are quite the opposite: no one but the doctors and nurses are allowed in; everyone is very clean to stop the patient getting infected; and every item of machinery and equipment is sterilised.

IN THE GENES

It takes 20,000 instructions, or genes, to make a human body. In future, we will understand more about genetics, how some genes cause certain illnesses and how they can also be used to cure others.

Added extras

20 YEARS

A person's genes do not really change throughout their life, but a recent discovery has found that extra molecules can become attached to DNA that boost the effect of certain genes. This process is called epigenetics, and it seems that it has a lot to do with our lifestyle. Healthy living boosts genes that protect the body, unhealthy habits do the opposite. In future, we may all take epigenetic medicines that keep our genes in tip-top working condition.

Sugar chain

Nucleic acid pair

IT'S ELEMENTARY

DNA

A body's genes are carried as a code on long molecule strands of DNA. DNA stands for deoxyribonucleic acid. 'Deoxyribo' refers to the two long spirals of sugar chains that DNA molecules are made of; 'nucleic acid' refers to repeated pairs of molecules strung between the sugar chains. Together they make a shape like a twisted ladder, also called 'double helix'. The DNA code is set out by the order of the nucleic acids that hold the sugar chains together. Every body cell has a full set of genes. All the DNA in a body running end to end would reach 20 billion km!

PHARMING

10 YEARS

Genetic engineers can take a gene from one life form and add it to the DNA of another. One big success of this technique was putting the gene for human insulin (an important hormone used to control the sugar in the blood) into bacteria. The bacteria then made human insulin, which could be given to diabetics – people who cannot produce insulin themselves. In future, we will be able to genetically engineer food, so it contains medicines. This process is nicknamed pharming (from the words pharmaceutical, meaning drug, and farming). Just think -- eating a yoghurt might cure a headache, while a couple of tomatoes will get rid of a sore throat.

UPLOADING

GENOME 70%

Personal medicine

15 YEARS

Everyone has a unique set of genes, called their genome. In the years to come, we will know our exact genome — our complete set of instructions that makes us who we are. We could have the data stored on our mobile phone. When we need medicine, we could upload our genome at the doctor's or chemist's, and get the best cure for our specific genes — or even have medicine made especially for us.

PAUSE FOR THOUGHT

In a few cases, we have linked a certain gene to a certain disease — if you have the gene, you are very likely to suffer from the disease. If in future we all have our genes recorded, what would happen to the people with those disease-causing genes?

TREATING ORGANS

Some of the most vital organs are the heart, lungs, brain and liver. If one of these stops working, you cannot live for very long. The word 'vital' originally meant 'full of life', but now it also means 'essential'. How will future medical treatments look after these essential body parts?

Brain boost

30 YEARS

As we get older, our brains work more slowly. We forget things more easily and take more time to make up our minds about things. Scientists are figuring out how brain cells are connected, forming pathways that help recall memories and make decisions. When researchers know more, it may be possible to add electronic implants to replace the brain pathways that break down as we age.

Grow your own

20 YEARS

The vital organs of other animals, such as pigs, are not so different from our own. However, if we tried to replace a faulty human kidney with one from a pig, our immune system would destroy the organ in a matter of days, because it would register the organ as an invading object. Instead, the answer might be to change the pig's genes, so its organs develop in exactly the same way as humans' do, and don't get rejected by human bodies.

PAUSE FOR THOUGHT

For every person whose life is saved using an organ grown inside another animal, that animal must die. The donor animal was grown to supply its organs, but is it ok to kill an animal to save one or several human lives?

Building blocks

Medical researchers take a lot of interest in stem cells. All your body parts grew from these cells when you were developing inside your mother. However, once a cell becomes specialised, into muscle or bone for example, it can't change into anything else. That is why a body that has been badly damaged (for example by nerve or blood vessel injury that has lead to amputation) cannot mend itself. But if we can make new stem cells for a patient, the body could use them to heal itself.

IT'S ELEMENTARY

TYPES OF STEM CELLS

Stem cells are not all the same: some are more powerful, or potent, than others. A totipotent stem cell can be used to make any type of body cell – including another totipotent cell. However, before it can start making different body parts, the totipotent cell needs to turn into a pluripotent stem cell. Pluripotent cells cannot turn back into totipotent cells, but they can produce a range of specialist stem cells. These stem cells go on to form certain types of body cell, such as blood or nerves.

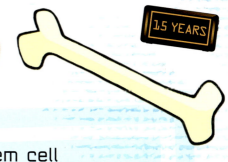

15 YEARS

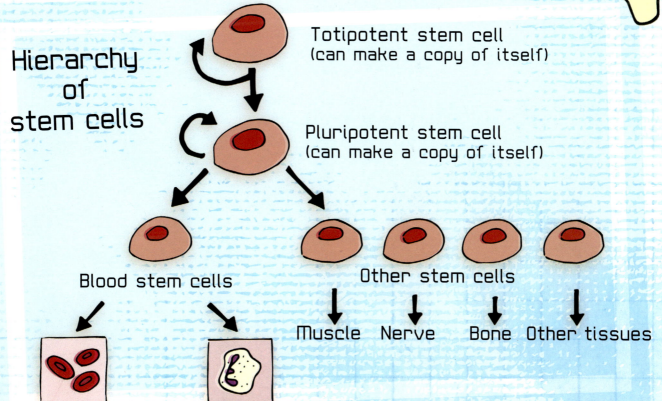

Hierarchy of stem cells

Totipotent stem cell (can make a copy of itself)

Pluripotent stem cell (can make a copy of itself)

Blood stem cells

Other stem cells

Muscle   Nerve   Bone   Other tissues

Red blood cells   White blood cells

NANOBOTS

You have probably heard of microscopic objects, such as a body cell or the electronic components on a microchip; but what about nanoscopic? Microscopic things are measured in millionths of a metre, while the nanoscale is measured in billionths. Machines this small might one day be at work inside our bodies, keeping us healthy.

Wireless connection

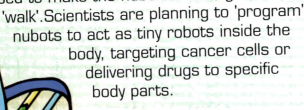

15 YEARS

We have all been 'going wireless' over the last few years, with our phones and computers sending and receiving information using Wifi, Bluetooth and other radio signals. Why not add some wireless technology to the human body? Radio signals from outside the body could send commands to nano devices inside. These could stimulate the brain to tackle depression, supply painkillers to injured areas, or control a nanobot to swim through your blood supply in order to fix a body part.

NUBOTS

30 YEARS

In future, tiny machines called nubots could be made from DNA itself. The body uses double strands of DNA to store our genes (see page 16). Now engineers are looking at ways of connecting several strands of DNA to produce 'mini machines' with arms, legs and pincers. DNA molecules can be 'programmed' to zip together in certain places and break apart in others. That process could be used to make the nubots move, grab other objects or even 'walk'. Scientists are planning to 'program' nubots to act as tiny robots inside the body, targeting cancer cells or delivering drugs to specific body parts.

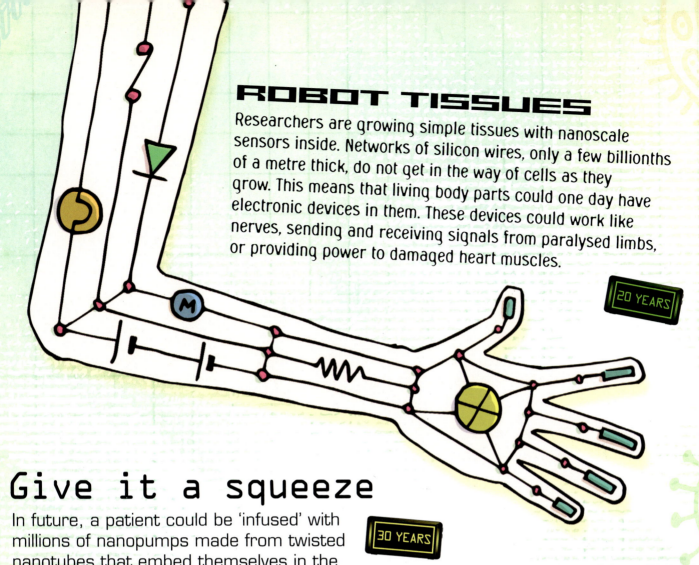

ROBOT TISSUES

Researchers are growing simple tissues with nanoscale sensors inside. Networks of silicon wires, only a few billionths of a metre thick, do not get in the way of cells as they grow. This means that living body parts could one day have electronic devices in them. These devices could work like nerves, sending and receiving signals from paralysed limbs, or providing power to damaged heart muscles.

20 YEARS

Give it a squeeze

In future, a patient could be 'infused' with millions of nanopumps made from twisted nanotubes that embed themselves in the body. In certain conditions, the pumps in the tubes could compress like a concertina, automatically pushing out medicines stored inside. If the conditions in the body changed, the pump would then lengthen and keep hold of the drug. Such a system could be set up in any body to supply a drug just where and when it is needed.

30 YEARS

IT'S ELEMENTARY

TAKE A TUBE

Nanotubes could change the world as we know it. They are tiny tubes made from hexagons of carbon atoms. They are super-lightweight but also incredibly strong (the strongest material ever made). A nanotube long enough to connect the Earth and the Moon would not break under its own weight, and if that same tube was rolled up, it would make a ball the size of a poppy seed! Just imagine what you could make with such a material.

SUPERSENSES

It is said that the human body has five senses: hearing, smell, taste, sight and touch. In fact, the human body senses in many more than five ways. For example, we feel heat, sense vibrations and experience pain. Technological advances might mean we could soon have many more ways of sensing what is happening in our bodies and in our environment. How will future science help us stay in touch with the world around us?

NOW!

Electronic eye

Light carries energy – the retina in our eyes converts that energy into nerve signals to send to the brain. A camera does something similar, only the energy is used to form a digital image. A miniature version of camera technology could allow some blind people to see. A sheet of tiny electronic light sensors is implanted on the faulty retina. Each sensor is 70 micrometres wide – not much bigger than the eye's own cells. The sensors pick up light and send a signal into the eye's nerve, just like the retina does. Normal light is too dim for the system to work, so users will wear goggles fitted with a camera. The images from the camera will be transmitted onto the implant in the eye, only much brighter so the sensors can pick it up.

STACKS OF FACTS

The retina is the light-sensitive layer in the eye.

Rods are used to see at night, in black and white; cones see in colour during the day.

The retina contains two types of cell, one shaped like rods the other more like cones.

The cone cells are clustered at the point right behind the pupil where the most detailed and colourful images are formed.

There are 125 million rod cells in the human eye. They are 100 times more sensitive to light than the cones.

BITTER TASTE

10 YEARS

It has been discovered that a bitter tastes boost the immune system. Germs in food can make it taste bitter, so taste serves as an early warning system for the body to prepare for an attack. In future, the same effect could be used to fool the body into fighting off a disease. A nasty bitter spray squirted up the nose would be all that is required to mobilise the immune system.

Smelling out problems

5 YEARS

One day it may be normal for a computer to smell your breath when you go to the doctor with a bad cough or lung infection. The computer can detect the whiff of different germs that are attacking your lungs and tell very quickly what medicines, if any, you need.

Ear power

5 YEARS

The days of hearing aids having battery packs hooked behind the ear may soon be over. A new hearing aid that is currently in development harnesses the electrical power produced by the nerves in the ear and surrounding muscles. The power supply is only tiny, but enough for a small hearing aid that fits right inside the ear.

RECYCLING TECHNOLOGY

Future medical advances might not all come from medical scientists. Other technologies of the future developed for non-medical reasons might end up being reused to save lives.

Silk-encased microchips melt away on contact with water.

SILK ELECTRONICS

Microchips or integrated circuits have revolutionised machines over the last 60 years. They may do the same for medicine. Ultrafine wires and other electronic components could be encased in silk fibres and stitched into the body. A simple device could be a heater, which warms an injury, killing bacteria and helping it to heal faster. And when its job is done, the silk disintegrates and the whole device melts away.

10 YEARS

Rescue robot

20 YEARS

Robots are not always copies of humans. Some of the strongest and fastest robots around today mimic animals such as dogs, beetles or dragonflies. In future, people injured in remote places could be saved by animal-like robots with the ability to climb, swim or jump to the rescue – and carry you to safety.

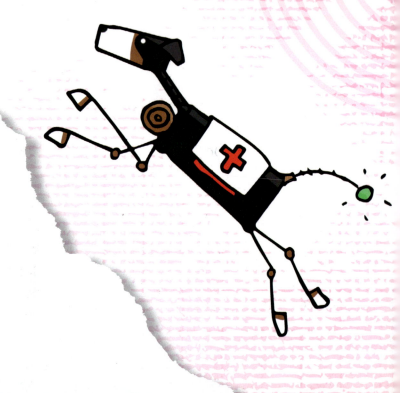

Voice diagnosis

Dementia is a serious condition in which a person's memory begins to fail, and they cannot remember how to look after themselves. Diagnosing the disease early helps to slow it down, and in future a voice test might help with this. A computer would look for unusual sounds in the voice that show dementia developing — you could be diagnosed down the phone!

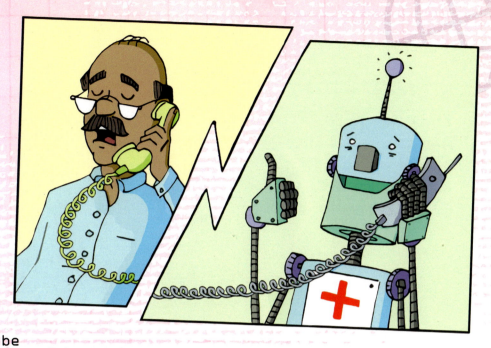

BREATHING LIQUID

Deep-sea divers might one day not breathe gas, but liquid. This would help them go deeper underwater than ever before. The liquid would be made of carbon and fluorine, with the oxygen that the body needs mixed into it. This means you could fill the lungs with it and not drown. The same liquid substitute for air could be used to treat people with damaged lungs, or help premature babies get strong enough to breathe air on their own, rather than needing a machine to help them.

Space surgery

If we send missions to Mars, space crews will spend many months in weightlessness – and that is a problem if they cut themselves or need simple surgery. Their blood and pus will float around the cabin and could infect the rest of the crew. One system being developed is to seal the wound in a watertight box and pump salty water over it, washing the blood away. A medic could then stitch up the wound using tools poking through into the box.

KEEPING FIT

They say that prevention is better than a cure, and we know that people who stay fit will also be healthy and suffer from fewer serious diseases later on in life. Technology will keep giving us smarter ways to keep our bodies healthy in future.

IN THE KNOW

10 YEARS

It is already possible to monitor body activity very closely, but it requires a lot of wires and gadgets. In future, miniature sensors in our clothes and homes or strapped to our skin will collect data more easily, for instance – what we eat, what exercise we do, and how long we sleep. A fitness app would then convert this information into advice about diet and taking exercise. Perhaps it would even tell us to put our feet up from time to time.

Stress app

5 YEARS

We all lose our temper every now and then, but when we are tired, worried or stressed we get angry more often. Long periods of stress can lead to illness, so an app on our phone listens to your voice patterns and warns you if you are getting too grumpy, too often. If so, it's time for a break.

Getting a buzz

Exercising and playing sport is not always good for your health. Many people pull muscles or injure themselves because they are not moving their body in the right way. Soon, smart sports gear will be filled with sensors that buzz if you are stretching too much or running in an inefficient way.

URBAN PLAYGROUND

Walking is great exercise, but we often prefer to go by car or catch a bus, even for short journeys. Towns of the future will be a lot more fun for pedestrians. Public spaces will contain interesting and playful objects for people to walk through and explore. Why take the lift when you can play music as you walk up the stairs, and why catch the bus when there are stepping stones and labyrinths running across town?

⚠ ERROR ALERT

Radium medicines

A century ago, people thought a newly discovered radioactive element called radium could make them healthy. Radium was added to toothpastes, tonic water and soaps. However, we now know that the radiation given out by radium is very dangerous. Nevertheless, because radium behaves in the same way as calcium, an element found in bones, it might be a good treatment for bone cancer in future. A new drug swaps the calcium in bones for radium, and the radiation it gives out stops the cancer from spreading.

FINDING ANSWERS

All medical innovations are the product of long and careful research. This will always be the case with future treatments, but scientists are coming up with new, clever ways to solve old problems.

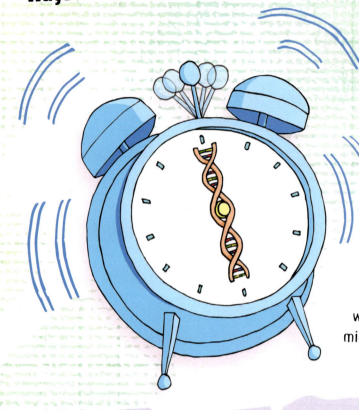

Everybody ageing

30 YEARS

There is one thing doctors cannot stop: people getting older. However, in future we might unlock how the body ages. A young body can normally mend itself completely, but older ones can't, and we begin to collect injuries and damage as we age. It might sound odd, but this does not have to be the case. It appears our genes have an in-built clock which means they can only be used a certain number of times – and that is why the body gradually stops working. If we can reset our genetic clocks, we might be able to live for much longer...

BODY ON A CHIP

10 YEARS

Studying how the body works is essential for figuring out new treatments, but being able to monitor what is going on inside the body is very hard to do. Scientists are beginning to grow body tissues, such as stomach linings, on top of microchips. The chips are fitted with a set of detectors that monitor the tissue's every activity. Implanted into the body, these chips will pass on valuable information to scientists about how different types of body tissue work.

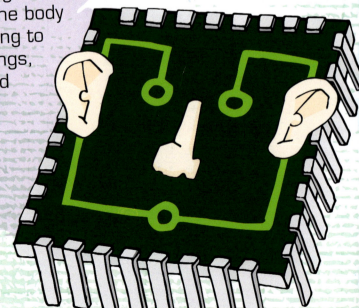

Making connections

Medical experts make sure they share their discoveries so they can all learn from each other's breakthroughs. Now all known chemicals – including those used as medicines – are being connected into a 'chemical internet'. What links the items of this huge computer database is information about how you make one chemical from another. Experts hope that all these connections will help them find new ways of making medicines and even see how new ones can be made in future.

`NOW!`

NON-GENE GENES

`15 YEARS`

Every gene's code is the building instructions for a specific protein molecule – proteins are used everywhere, from muscles to stomach enzymes. However, most of the DNA in the body is not a gene, as it does not contain any code. We used to think this DNA was just left-over junk, but the latest research suggests that it is really a set of switches that control the 'real' genes. Once we figure out how it all works, we might discover that serious diseases such as cancer and autism are caused by these mysterious bits of DNA.

PAUSE FOR THOUGHT

Modern medicine can cure many diseases that might have killed our great-grandparents and so people today can live to a great age. Although we are living longer, many of us will spend our older years suffering from a long list of medical complaints. Is it always better to cure someone, or perhaps there is a time to let them die naturally?

GLOSSARY

3-D Short for three-dimensional; when a flat picture on a screen (or even paper) is presented in such a way that it looks like it is a real object, with length and width, but also depth.

ailment Another word for illness or problem with the body, normally a non-serious one.

atom The smallest building block of a material. There are about 90 types of atom found on Earth, which combine to make all the things we see around us, including our bodies.

blood pressure A measure of how hard the heart is pushing blood around the body. Low blood pressure makes people feel faint, while high blood pressure weakens the heart.

cancer A serious disease where the body's growth system goes wrong and unwanted lumps, or tumours, develop inside the body and damage healthy parts.

cyber To do with computers.

data A collection of measurements or other useful numbers.

depression A common illness with many causes in which a person finds it hard to feel happy.

diagnosis The process a doctor uses to figure out what is wrong with a person.

digital To record or represent something in terms of numbers or digits. Only two digits are used 1 and 0.

electron A tiny particle found inside atoms and also the means of carrying electricity; electric currents are a flow of electrons.

endoscope A machine for inserting a flexible camera inside the body, either through the mouth, via the anus or through a cut made in the body.

fluorine An element found in many rocks.

fungi A major type of life; fungi include yeast and mushrooms.

gene Something that can be inherited, or passed down from parents to children. The gene is transmitted in the form of DNA.

genetic To do with genes.

implants An artificial (or non-natural) object that is added to the body.

microscope A device for looking up close at small objects.

obesity To be very overweight so that health is affected.

paralysed To be unable to move part of the body.

pharmacology The science of medicines.

prognosis A prediction a doctor makes on how quickly a patient will get better.

pus A liquid made of dead body cells that fill cuts and wounds when they get infected.

radioactive A material that has unstable atoms; as the atoms break apart they give out dangerous radiation that can damage the body.

retina The light-sensitive layer at the back of the eye.

symptoms The outward signs that a person has a disease.

technology Using scientific knowledge to make useful tools.

ultrasonic Sound that is very, very high pitched, far too high for humans to hear.

venom A poison produced by an animal and injected into victims in a bite or sting.

X-ray A high-energy and invisible form of light that shines right through soft body parts.

USEFUL WEBSITES:

Find about about nanobots, the miniature machines of the future, from the scientists who are making them.:
http://www.youtube.com/watch?v=7wuujmiqD-w

Some prosthetics that are in use today are already incredibly high-tech:
http://www.youtube.com/watch?v=_qUPnnROxvY

Despite modern medicine there are still many medical problems to solve in future. Check out the World Clock to see life and death in numbers:
http://www.poodwaddle.com/clocks/worldclock/

INDEX